NATURE'S CYCLES

A CHICKEN'S LIFE CYCLE

A.B. CLAMANT

NORWOOD HOUSE PRESS

Cataloging-in-Publication Data

Names: Clamant, A.B., 1972-.
Title: A chicken's life cycle / A.B. Clamant.
Description: Buffalo, NY : Norwood House Press, 2026. | Series: Nature's cycles | Includes glossary and index.
Identifiers: ISBN 9781978575523 (pbk.) | ISBN 9781978575530 (library bound) | ISBN 9781978575547 (ebook)
Subjects: LCSH: Chickens--Life cycles--Juvenile literature.
Classification: LCC SF487.5 C536 2026 | DDC 598.6'25--dc23

Published in 2026 by
Norwood House Press
2544 Clinton Street
Buffalo, NY 14224

Designer: Rhea Magaro
Editor: Kim Thompson

Photo credits: Cover, p. 1 Majna/Shutterstock.com; p. 3 PeopleImages.com- Yuri A/Shutterstock.com; p. 5 Wassana Panapute, fukume/Shutterstock.com; p. 6 Svetlana Orusova/Shutterstock.com; p. 7 Alter-egop. 8 Anastasia Magonova/Shutterstock.com; p. 11 annushka_k/Shutterstock.com; p. 14 TEA OOR/Shutterstock.com; p. 15 Ton Bangkeaw/Shutterstock.com; pp. 16, 17 Budimir Jevtic/Shutterstock.com; p. 18 TTstudio/Shutterstock.com; p. 19 Sarah Macor/Shutterstock.com; p. 21 TarraPatta /Shutterstock.com

Printed in the United States of America

CPSIA compliance information: Batch #CSNHP26: For further information contact Norwood House Press at 1-800-237-9932.

TABLE OF CONTENTS

Where Do Chickens Come From? 4

The Chicken Dance 6

The Incredible Egg 10

Time to Hatch 14

The Cycle Continues 18

Glossary 22

Thinking Questions 23

Index 24

About the Author 24

Where Do Chickens Come From?

A **rooster** struts and pecks. An egg is hard and still. The two things have nothing to do with each other, right? Wrong! They are both part of the amazing life **cycle** of chickens.

The Chicken Dance

A chicken's life begins with a dance. A rooster prances around a **hen** to get her attention.

The hen and the rooster come together to **mate**. The next day, the hen goes to her nest. She lays a **fertilized** egg.

A hen can lay an egg once a day. Eggs can be fertilized or unfertilized. Nothing will grow inside an unfertilized egg. Inside a fertilized egg, a new life can begin.

The Incredible Egg

After she lays eggs, a hen feels broody. That means she wants to sit on her eggs and protect them. Her feathers keep the eggs warm. The eggs will **incubate** for 20 or 21 days.

An **embryo** forms inside the egg. The embryo eats the egg's **yolk**. The yolk is loaded with **nutrients**.

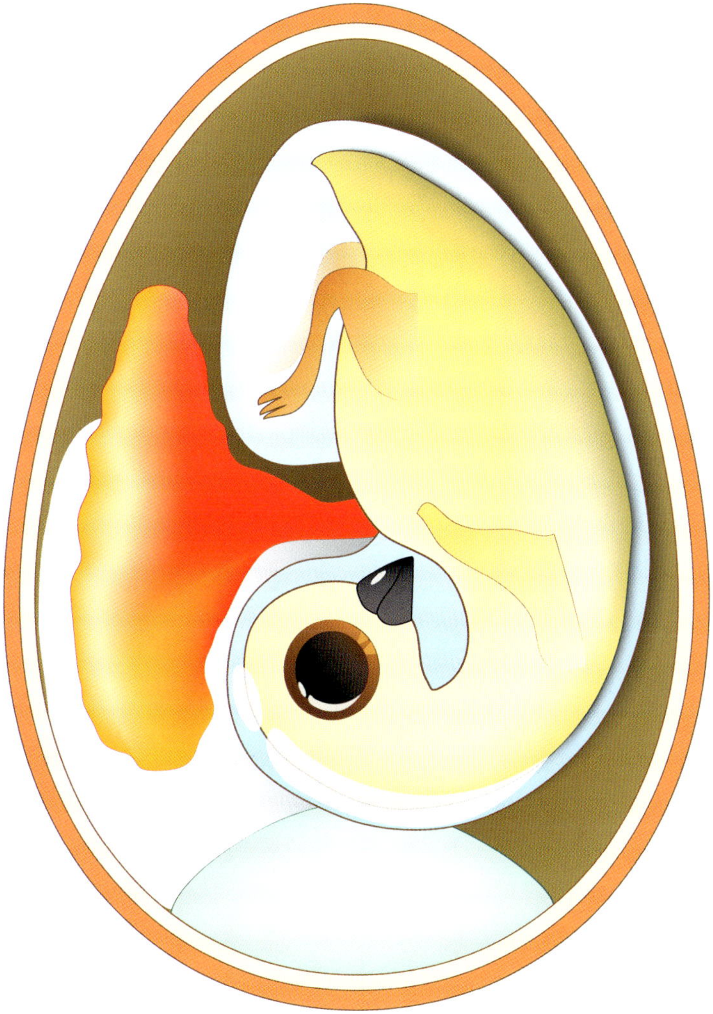

The embryo grows bigger. It becomes a chick.
Soon, it gets too crowded in there!

Time to Hatch

The chick is ready to **hatch**. Its beak has a sharp tip called an egg tooth. It uses the egg tooth to tap on the egg's shell. It taps thousands of times until it breaks through.

It takes a few hours for the chick to slowly come out. It is tired. Cracking an egg open from the inside is hard work!

In a few hours, the baby chicks are dry and fluffy. They begin to move around.

The Cycle Continues

As a chick grows, its egg tooth falls off. Its feathers come in.

After six months, chickens are fully grown. The adult hens and roosters are ready to mate. The life cycle begins again.

Have you ever wondered about which came first, the chicken or the egg? Now you know they are both part of a chicken's amazing life cycle.

Glossary

cycle (SYE-kuhl): a series of events that repeat over and over in the same order

embryo (EM-bree-oh): an unborn baby

fertilized (FUR-tuh-lized): able to grow into a new life because mating has occurred, and male and female parts have joined together

hatch (hach): to break out of an egg to be born

hen (hen): an adult female chicken

incubate (ING-kyuh-bate): kept warm enough to grow and develop

mate (mate): the pairing of a male and female to produce babies

nutrients (NOO-tree-uhntz): substances that living things need to grow and stay healthy, such as proteins, vitamins, and minerals

rooster (ROO-stur): an adult male chicken

yolk (yoke): the yellow part inside an egg that is used to feed a growing embryo

Thinking Questions

1. How often can hens lay eggs?
2. What is a fertilized egg?
3. What do chicken embryos eat?
4. How do eggs stay warm?
5. How long does it take for chicks to become adult chickens?

Index

adult 19

egg tooth 14, 18

eggs 4, 7, 9, 10, 12, 14, 15, 20

embryo 12, 13

feathers 10, 18

hens 6, 7, 9, 10, 19

incubate 10

mate 7, 19

roosters 4, 6, 7, 19

shell 14

About the Author

A.B. Clamant is the author of several fact-filled books for kids. The daughter of two grade school teachers, she developed a love of children's books at an early age. When she's not writing, she is working on opening her own petting zoo, ABCs Animals. Her favorite foods are bread, fruit strips, and candy. A.B. Clamant lives in Springfield, Missouri, with her four cats: Monkey, Corky, Prissy, and Nelly.